EXHALATION HALVES LAMBDA

poems by

Julia Rose Lewis

Finishing Line Press
Georgetown, Kentucky

EXHALATION HALVES LAMBDA

Copyright © 2017 by Julia Rose Lewis
ISBN 978-1-63534-180-5 First Edition
All rights reserved under International and Pan-American Copyright Conventions.
No part of this book may be reproduced in any manner whatsoever without written permission from the publisher, except in the case of brief quotations embodied in critical articles and reviews.

ACKNOWLEDGMENTS

The Gambler Mag - The House Wins: "Re: Break, Make Or After Dora Malech", "In Medias Res"
Vagabonds: Anthology of the Mad Ones: "Against Horses, Against Writing"
Backlash Volume 2: "Untitled"
The Title is Elusive: "Steps to an Ecology of Mind", "Body Forces", "Witch Timing"
3am Magazine: "In the Middle of Dishes", "Monkeys, Humans, and Whales Oh My!"
Oddball Magazine: "Sevenling for Yesterday Morning", "Dear Biologist",
Re:Visions: "Re: Where Are Your Dreams Turtle?"
GTK: "Swelling with Water"
Sparks of Consciousness: "Breaking Again", "Of Cats and Bathtubs", "Re: Water's Monologue", "You Were the Discoverer of the Wormhole to the Gamma Quadrant.", "Nolite Te Bastardes Carborundorum (Margaret Atwood)"
Lumina Poetry Contest 3rd place: "Is This Dissonance?", "Re: Dream of Moss and Red Eft", "Re: Pent up Musings"

Publisher: Leah Maines

Editor: Christen Kincaid

Cover Art: Julia Rose Lewis

Author Photo: Mark Mattoon

Cover Design: Elizabeth Maines McCleavy

Printed in the USA on acid-free paper.
Order online: www.finishinglinepress.com
        also available on amazon.com

        Author inquiries and mail orders:
        Finishing Line Press
        P. O. Box 1626
        Georgetown, Kentucky 40324
        U. S. A.

Table of Contents

Sevenling for Yesterday Morning 1
Untitled 2
Dear Biologist 3
Is This Dissonance? 4
Steps to an Ecology of Mind 5
Re: Dream of Moss and Red Eft 6
The Future Library Project 7
Breaking Again 8
Re: Pent Up Musings 9
Water and tub are an island of water in a dry house 10
Re: Make, Break, Or After Dora Malech 11
Witch Timing 12
Re: Water's Monologue 13
You Were the Discoverer of the Wormhole to the
    Gamma Quadrant 14
Re: Harping On 15
Of Cats and Bathtubs 16
Row Your Bathtub 17
Body Forces 18
Swelling with Water 19
Tau Is the Greek Numeral for Three-Hundred 20
Monkeys, Humans, and Whales Oh My! 21
In Medias Res 22
Exhalation Half Lingering 23
Against Horses, Against Writing 24
Re: Where Are Your Dreams Turtle? 25
Nolite Te Bastardes Carborundorum (Margaret Atwood) 26
Recipe for a Summer 27
In the Middle of Dishes 29

to AS

Sevenling for Yesterday Morning

A bit of strawberry buried in the sand,
a handstand held longer under water and,
a ferry passed

my salt matted hair.
Your thumbs passing over were so much bigger,
the profile, the shadow, the closeness of your Adam's apple.

How did you wait for the dampness to dry away?

Untitled

The poet's answer:

Yes, Adam can cast a shadow. Shadows are good, beautiful. Truth and beauty and negative ca-pability, Keats casts a shadow over us.

The chemist's answer:

In 2012, a group at the University of Brisbane was able to demonstrate the absorption imaging of a single atom of ytterbium by laser. "A single atom scattering resonant light can closely approach these limits, making it an excellent test system for investigating fundamental limits to imaging... In particular, the dynamics of chromatin in living cells [13] could be imaged without delivering a lethal UV dose." I have printed out a copy of the paper, if you would like to read it.

A third of an answer:

Both scientists and poets should be careful of gratuitous acts of anthropomorphisation and per-sonification. It is something that I am playing with in my dissertation. I would like to see you. Maybe here?

Dear Biologist,

Please help me.

Are you real?
Can I touch you, please?
I have proved objective reality with a tea kettle.

The tea kettle hasn't caught fire yet I am burning.

Is This Dissonance?

The mosquito was not afraid.

I saw it fly, perfect spirals form,
across the table.

The mosquito was too far from your
ear for you to hear its whine.

I was too far from forming it.

The gray warped boards of the table
wave, we're too wide.

I am frayed.

Steps to an Ecology of Mind

Things get in a muddle.
times got in a muddle

time is gotten a muddle
time I'd given a mud idle
time I'd gained a mud idle
time I'd gained a mud I land
time I'd gained a mud island
time I'd gained a mad isle
time I'd gamed my hand isle
time I'm game my hand isle
time I'm game my sand isle
time I'm game my I sand I'll blue

time I'm game my I sand I love you
Time, I'm game, my I said, "I love you."

Re: Dream of Moss and Red Eft

A pair of red and spotted newts reside in his now growing eyes. Gold, and orange remember efts two chambered heart outgrew has turned into three chambered heart for my traveling far to ponds or rivers lives. The efts so often nocturnal yet active they eat land snails and sea snails for novelty, on rainy days. When one can only see some mirroring blue or pewter water blurring against gold and brown. My yellow wish inside the mud bottoms glowing red efts, red depths, remember the red droplets, yes?

Do not put eastern newts in nuclear magnetic resonance imagers, western ones not known.

The Future Library Project

They used to be
trees,

a copse.
There was a sacrifice

once the botanist read the tree rings.
Leaves lying.

This is dissonance.
Life after life,

dear trees,
are books better than applesauce?

I have surrounded myself with corpses; I am in heaven.

Breaking Again

"Tell me a story…"
Lighthousekeeping

Thank you for taking me to the Moth last night. I do have money for you for my ticket. I'm sorry I forgot to give it to you.

Will's breaking project essay is as much a reflection of him as you as me. I am beginning to break old habits.

At the start of my life and at the start of the summer, I said no to you. I held you at a distance. How does a double negative mean differently than a yes? I think double negative implies change and counterfactuals. Not no, in silence's stead.

I am afraid you will break my brain, the red and gray place in my head.

Holding Pattern is the name of a series of poems in my dissertation. They are old love poems (baltic isopods). I have been avoiding them this summer. They need revision, I know, but I was afraid of confronting old feelings. I have been avoiding the old man (object) of the poems as well. He is on island; we have been friends. After listening to you last night, I feel less afraid. Even braided and soldered sterling silver will unravel now and again.

I love how responsive you are to my writing. I love how responsive your body is to mine. I love that you said, "Descartes was wrong," in bed.

"This is not a love story, but love is in it. That is, love is just outside it, looking for a way to break in."
Lighthousekeeping

Re: Pent Up Musings

So you say, not the silvers, all the forest and the fjords. The breed that I have loved from Norway. Yet western the golden horse with light the feather rings on lower legs and full length dorsal stripe. For slight this draft to march the heart and match the hair to braid around. They have the tale halefjær the oldest breed at viking burial sites. A slight draft opposite of your narrow and lengthy waterbody. I have explored for fjords are deeper than the nearby sea. Bring truth and beauty be the golden mean.

Water and tub are an island of water in a dry house.
After Matthea Harvey

Bathtub: Dear wait, where?
Water: You with the firm white skin, dear bathtub.

Bathtub: Found in soaking.
Water: Dear rest tub.

Bathtub: Biologists know that short is the time of the toad soaking.
Water: Do rest up.

Bathtub: Find the boundary.
Water: I used to pity the bathtub its forced embrace of the human form.

Bathtub: Hot soap?
Water: No, not soap, but the title of a poem.

Bathtub: Because sometimes you clean me.
Water: Is soap the baby, so hope, so much soap, still a small ball?

Bathtub: Found out.
Water: I have seen no being with bright red legs.

Bathtub: I will be holding my depth.
Water: Do not fear rest open.

Bathtub: Feeling not fear ring.
Water: Dramatic is the introduction of ducklings to my depths.

Bathtub: Oh, my water is boiling.
Water: I will be right back world.

Re: Break, Make Or
> *After Dora Malech*

At yeast the gist, you tried to rescue the peas from drowning. Old lifeguard, with toast trying to reach me, out across the sea. With marmite, I felt, I see now butter and peas both brown unseemly might. An eye is boiling over, and hissing head is held in screen and gloves. Oh yes the peas like gold and green apples for cold October fare. Your face had frozen when you were carrying me, your tortured time. I felt you place the laptop by the toaster, not cultured butter please! But evil butter, green the craving turns to yellow craving. The bread was spread before you to dream of frozen peas and salted sweet cream butter.

Witch Timing

Wish, wash, wait.

In which he wraps his hands
around my waist.

I want to rub olive oil into his hands
and
add crushed red chili flakes for him
to red the oil
"red deeps"
I picture the bottle of
rust-red hot sauce on his kitchen table.

I have watched him take.

Re: Water's Monologue

This is the character of water wanting inside the tree where apples are happening; they are bathtub white now. Because the body is not only pipe, nor pump, I must worry about pollution. A cup of tea being a bathtub in miniature some bitterness, same the heat. Here I reside in Nantucket's tap as great the glasses of water or lakes, a thinking cup its breaking point.

Of capricorns, Enki, and I besides the biologist likes the goats; they give their milk, the fish for dinner oven ready ocean. His voice across the Atlantic reading to me. I want to be an island of water inside the dry this horse a Sagittarius yes.

You Were the Discoverer of the Wormhole to the Gamma Quadrant
After Bianca Stone

Gamma is the Greek number three: you, me, and Dax (Lela, Tobin, Emony, Audrid, Torias, Joran, Curzon, Jadzia, and Ezri, the joined thrill.)

You run anomaly scans in operations at night to relax. I check you for ticks because you are extremely allergic to insect bites.

Your favorite drink is a Black Hole and your unrequited love was a physicist. The teacher, the explorer, the biologist, the fourth is not given.

Your mentor tried to steal the body of a shape-shifter decades after he washed you out of the program. Still, you miss the *hoobishan* baths at home.

You look good in blue. In vessels named for the earth's rivers the Gander, Ganges, Mekong, Orinoco, Rio Grande, Rubicon, Shenandoah, Volga, Yangtzee Kiang, and Yukon.

You have inherited a love of steamed, not fried, nor sauteed, *azna* from prior hosts. I dislike okra of all kinds.

You are attracted to aliens, *farangi* (a Persian word), and sleeping in the skins of animals slaughtered on a alien world.

You commanded the defiant.
Run you boat.

You are late; we schedule our time together in twenty-six hour days. Where do you see yourself in three-hundred years?

I would like to see some of my molecules and some of your molecules in the runabout Rio Grande. Watch the emissary and what you leave behind to understand you are loved.

Re: Harping On

The story of my medieval history teacher on nobles, horses, falcons, lyres, and fingers. "She hopes someday to learn to play the harp," to play with air and strings. Compress the air, so sing the longest minstrel's tale my dear, the pitch the note is signed, the book I keep. Why are harps shaped the way they are? A named shape, the triangle is equilateral, a nabla, a harp, an upside down delta. One need not use the hardest physics, understand, the Navier-Stokes equations here for harps. So nabla dot is divergence. Is there dissonance? It is my english teacher, deserving an accordion she deserves to spend the rest of time struggling.

Of Cats and Bathtubs

The flattest sentences I could find. Four and ten are fourteen. Four times ten is forty. The verb to be in poetry, the equals sign in mathematics, metaphor really, where is the mountain in the photograph? The leg of a horse can be a cliff face to a kitten, the thickness of a draft horse.

Be kind nightmare. There is nothing delicate about this old warmblood.

The flat test I created for you.

When I am with you, *Mu* is equivalent to *Enki*. *Mu* is forty. *Enki* is forty. Force the mouse to sing. This is the story of a cat named Mouse. First named *Mu*, his brother *Pi* died, and so his name changed. He was the mewling kitten. Now the muse singing.

The kitten that did not get killed.

Mu rhymes with new. Nu is the flow velocity. Nu is a variable in the Navier-Stokes equation for de-scribing fluid behavior. Remember *Enki* is the god of water and semen. Where are the other verbs?

The floating rest here.

Row Your Bathtub

Hold tight the
One opposite a boat.

Rock in the sea, I land. In harbor
Here are rose hard roe
Of salmon only.

Roe of scallops are not Kosher remember.
Humor and food fried in
Oil of course!

Read the red temperature,
Hope the fluid behaves right for the
Onions now.

Rho,
Hekaton,
One-hundred.

Body Forces

Arc, or bowing creature on tests
the blood, the fluids, people fear
undercooked venison to be, host.

Testing the flatness of sentences.
The whiteness it is fur, the kitten
was not flat, it was a misreading,

for he is simply not a cat person.

Swelling with Water

From the heart to the feet,
bare soak king
press sure and hard. Breathing,

balancing,
I was doing the point thing in clogs, rings
of blisters from the feet. To the heart

I remember falling,
asleep at the barre.
Stretching my left leg, press sore,

lifting
my leg off. Flailing
from the heart to the feet

finding myself, caught in blankets.
He said, he found ballet like foot binding
because pressure is force over area.

He said, he thought I was taller.
All I wanted, sweating
from the feet to the heart,
to press ourselves pleasing.

Tau is the Greek Numeral for Three-Hundred

Upper case tea, will there be any bergamot
in three-hundred years? I cry through my nose.
Oil of bitter orange skin, these trees afloat
in warm acidic water. We are now how close?

Red the deeps of *Monardia didyma* she dreams
and is dumb. How do hummingbirds see
color? Red (not purple) the ragged bright streams
and brownish bracts are Oswego tea.

I am the green leaves and purple of herb
(not orange) the wild mint, horse mint, is
mentha citrata. When you disturb
it, stress it, it goes pale and tenser, bliss or miss?

Olive oil, garlic powder, zucchini, and peppers
here we are green and purple again with tea stained papers.

Monkeys, Humans, and Whales Oh My!

The measure of rope sleeping deep inside your pack, wife of monstrosity. In the middle of Moby Dick is the chapter Monkey-Rope. This red try heels out of depth. Look down there blood the sharks their jaws. Bound by hemp, the harpooner is treasure his waist to weight.

Monkey cope; we are wedded by rope. Wife of brain calculate the bulk viscosity, lambda, the blubber the sperm whale was hunted. Posterior to anterior, *lambda* plus *spandrel* equals whale. Or change the variable from bulk viscosity to pressure.

To walk the beach monkey-armed, reaching out to trash. With fingers featuring plastics off white or gray or yellow. Do not rotate your big toes. So duh, better the biologist you were. The dead thing, half in the soda can that was so pungent, what was it? Remember the stone you found the night we had wild and not salmon for dinner? The monkey-rose is salmon roe as miniature pink lady apples.

Dear brain of monkey, I played with your words. Retreading the monkey toes are caudal as the heal. Sound the answer out. What creature leaves its tracks for longer than a minute in water? A stone skipped, man swimming. It drinks, the creature takes the water inside itself. To fall is how the water loves you.

In Medias Res

(is a river)	is a shovel-nosed snake in which it	(trace of itself)
(wave)	travels through I myself-fluidized	(half human)
(and wave)	flew it I did side the thing is sand	(my body)
(stressed as tau)	happens sheared from the head to	(half horse)
(squamate)	the tail, the long among my grain	(the slender plan)
(hard science)	soft materials is in which sand is	(following velocity)
(golden in water)	happening flow the body swims	(half snake)

Exhalation Half Lingering

I am mesh
of human lungs
lay by the airway
walls, the bronchial
trees, the field is fluid;
domain is mine. Deformation
tensor here displacement, density.
Any given lung has velocity inflow
and pressure outflow. Did you know
germans rotate the colon 900
and place it over a "d"
symbol to indicate
the second
derivative.

A method for
solving the time-
dependent Navier-
Stokes equations,
aiming at higher Reynolds'
number, is presented here.
For this purpose assume human
lungs are non-superimposable
mirror images. I am
missing. Mesh is
deformed by
body force.
Think stress
tensor.

Against Horses, Against Writing

I suspect I am guilty of confusing writing with life. Of believing that as the writing was good, so life was good. But writing always fails to imitate life. We are defined by our failure to imitate those who we ad-mire. Writing is showing not telling or only a little telling. One shows a horse that they love it; you are more than a centaur. The truth about love stories is that they must be told. I must tell you in person; I love you. I love this life with you.

Yes, writing is an important part still. I love the smell of roast chicken because of you. I love waking up so close. I love your love of zucchini, all things green. I crave you like avocado. In all the concrete de-tails, we are told are important, it is easy to forget to tell. I let myself be derailed from telling you. Well lived and well-loved are only a letter apart. What I love about you, are all the things I can not show to others. That place where we two meet, *serendib*, Sri Lanka, remember the frog poem. You are there.

There is adventure in depth as well as breadth. The distance between start and end points, building. All relationships end in death or break up. Before, every year is a new year. Every day is different as a fjord. Every day is unpredictably lavish and challenging. Against horses, against writing; there is our life.

It is terrifying to give up control of oneself, one's life to another person. Insecurity comes in the form of difference. Insecurity gives rise to distance. We think, yes we, they are too different. I can not trust an-other with my life as they will not make the decisions I would. That is the rub, the friction is that which gives rise to heat. I want to keep you warm. I love your differences; they will grow me. You will grow me, if I let you. I will grow you, if you let me.

Re: Where Are Your Dreams Turtle?

Yes, turtles, I will try! Inside my dreams, outside the world, not Gertrude Stein, when I a turtle the word is my own designed shell. The world is resting on the turtle's shell not snails, not whelks, not scallops, not quahogs. The scallopers haircut has coming fallen I will to home for fried and sautéed scallops from carapace to car. To tent to coat to box-ers, not box turtles, but sawback turtles, like maps their carapace markings. There is a turtle tall enough for me to rest my head on flatness, his is soft (his chest) and listen. Giantest turtle, what do you feel about rivers? All right rivers.

Nolite Te Bastardes Carborundorum
(Margaret Atwood)

Nolite
Polite
Not lie
No light (not quite black hole)
Night life (magic)

Te
(Tea)
Thee
The
Thou

Bastardes
Bastards!

Carborundorum
Car bore run door rum
Cardboard and or um (some)
Cared or under hum
Carbon dear come home (soon)

From sand and water come castles. Here is calcium carbonate from scallop shells and silicon dioxide on the ground. Sand paper grinds you down, yes, and polishes. The shine and electrical properties of silicon carbide can be mistaken for diamond.

From sand and water come quicksand. You live with the grit of fallen sandcastles. The water will wash you for a time.

Recipe for a Summer

It was the summer of my love affair with garlic, and I grew into a connoisseur of the caesar salad. I would suffer neither chicken nor shrimp on top. The lemon wedge I always transferred to my bread plate. The crouton is the brain of the dish; it tells all. No salt should ever be added to the salad as the anchovies carry the salt. The shaved parmesan still cast shadows over lettuce, green on green on white. I stuck my fork into the lettuce instead of talking to the strange nurse at the table. The plate obsessed me. Before my father had twirled lettuce on a fork like pasta, when we ate at the Jared Coffin House.

To turn out the plate:

Dress the heads of Romaine lettuce
Add the croutons into the mixture above
Shave the parmesan over all
Place anchovies on top of the parmesan
Finish with a lemon wedge for garnish

When the only fruit is Florida citrus, let this. January is the month of Italian food and the beginning of the infernal rains on island. You were enjoying your mother's Christmas present, rain pants. My mother and I order Caesar salads, timid, you follow suit. The whitest dressings use mayonnaise, and too much turns the taste into the blandest ranch dressing. Although almost all salad dressings have an emulsified ingredient, not all dressings are emulsions. A classical Caesar appears yellow, wish the egg yoke and mustard smooth together.

Undressing, you tell me how delicately my mother and I eat.

What to dress the lettuce with:

good mild olive oil
freshly squeezed lemon juice
freshly grated parmesan cheese
anchovy paste
egg yoke
and/or
dijon mustard

Fit the food processor with a steel blade. Place the egg yolk, mustard, garlic, anchovies, lemon juice, and pepper into the bowl of the food processor. Process the mixture until smooth. With the processor running, pour the olive oil through the feed tube as though you were making mayonnaise. Continue processing until thick, think semen. Add grated parmesan and pulse three times.

Let us dress and thus dressed sing. Our style is defined by our failure to imitate those who we admire. Meanwhile, you juggle the remaining lemons in the dining room. Even this motion means sweating in July.

In the Middle of Dishes

After the soap and water, after the wire brush,
after the acetone, after the soak, there is white

hard matter attached to the (old) glassware, in
the micro-distillation kits. So I test the longer

stir bar in one liter of de-ionized water, before
measuring into six weigh boats, the potassium

hydroxide. Add (one) on the half hour, wait to
return to room temperature. Repeat five times.

Add the aqueous potassium hydroxide, to four
liters isopropyl alcohol. Add the round bottom

flasks, 25mL 50mL, to the base bath tub. Rest
and washed remember those dishes await you.

Then open the door, to dry the laundry semen-
less (and god said light) *dixitque deum lumen*.

Julia Rose Lewis is a poet and scientist who divides her time between Nantucket island and the United Kingdom. In 2010, she received her bachelors degree in Biology and Chemistry from Bryn Mawr College. She received her MFA in Creative Writing from Kingston University in 2015.

From 2015-2016 she was poet-in-residence with the Archeology Department at the University of Wales Trinity Saint David. She is a member of the Moors Poetry Collective and her poems have appeared in their anthologies. Her poems have appeared in *3AM Magazine, Enchanting Verses, The Missing Slate, Poetry Wales*. She is co-organizer of the Cardiff Poetry Experiment reading series. Her chapbook, *Zeroing Event* (2016), was published by Zarf Poetry.

www.ingramcontent.com/pod-product-compliance
Lightning Source LLC
LaVergne TN
LVHW041506070426
835507LV00012B/1368